LUTHER'S
SMALL CATECHISM

Intersynodical
Translation

Printing Statement:

Due to the very old age and scarcity of this book, many of the pages may be hard to read due to the blurring of the original text, possible missing pages, missing text and other issues beyond our control.

Because this is such an important and rare work, we believe it is best to reproduce this book regardless of its original condition.

Thank you for your understanding.

LUTHER'S

SMALL CATECHISM

Martin Luther
Born Nov. 10, 1483; died Feb. 18, 1546

DR. MARTIN LUTHER'S
SMALL CATECHISM
1529

Intersynodical Translation

ADOPTED BY
THE EVANGELICAL LUTHERAN AUGUSTANA SYNOD
OF NORTH AMERICA
1929

*The five parts, with a selection
of occasional prayers*

AUGUSTANA BOOK CONCERN
ROCK ISLAND, ILLINOIS

AUGUSTANA BOOK CONCERN
ROCK ISLAND, ILL.
1948

PART I
THE TEN COMMANDMENTS

THE INTRODUCTION
I am the LORD thy God.

THE FIRST COMMANDMENT
Thou shalt have no other gods before Me.

What does this mean?

Answer: We should fear, love, and trust in God above all things.

THE SECOND COMMANDMENT
Thou shalt not take the Name of the LORD thy God in vain; for the LORD will not hold him guiltless that taketh His Name in vain.

What does this mean?

Answer: We should fear and love God so that we do not curse, swear, conjure, lie, or deceive, by His Name, but call upon Him in every time of need, and worship Him with prayer, praise, and thanksgiving.

THE THIRD COMMANDMENT

Remember the Sabbath day, to keep it holy.

What does this mean?

Answer: We should fear and love God so that we do not despise His Word and the preaching of the same, but deem it holy, and gladly hear and learn it.

THE FOURTH COMMANDMENT

Honor thy father and thy mother, that thy days may be long upon the land which the LORD thy God giveth thee.

What does this mean?

Answer: We should fear and love God so that we do not despise our parents and superiors, nor provoke them to anger, but honor, serve, obey, love, and esteem them.

THE FIFTH COMMANDMENT
Thou shalt not kill.

What does this mean?

Answer: We should fear and love God so that we do our neighbor no bodily harm nor cause him any suffering, but help and befriend him in every need.

THE SIXTH COMMANDMENT
Thou shalt not commit adultery.

What does this mean?

Answer: We should fear and love God so that we lead a chaste and pure life in word and deed, and that husband and wife love and honor each other.

THE SEVENTH COMMANDMENT
Thou shalt not steal.

What does this mean?

Answer: We should fear and love God so that we do not rob our neighbor of his money or property, nor bring them into our possession by unfair dealing or fraud, but help him to improve and protect his property and living.

THE EIGHTH COMMANDMENT

Thou shalt not bear false witness against thy neighbor.

What does this mean?

Answer: We should fear and love God so that we do not deceitfully belie, betray, backbite, nor slander our neighbor, but apologize for him, speak well of him, and put the most charitable construction on all that he does.

THE NINTH COMMANDMENT

Thou shalt not covet thy neighbor's house.

What does this mean?

Answer: We should fear and love God so that we do not seek by craftiness to gain possession of our neighbor's inheritance or home nor obtain them under pretense of a legal right, but assist and serve him in keeping the same.

The Tenth Commandment

Thou shalt not covet thy neighbor's wife, nor his manservant, nor his maidservant, nor his cattle, nor anything that is thy neighbor's.

What does this mean?

Answer: We should fear and love God so that we do not estrange or entice away our neighbor's wife, servants, or cattle, but seek to have them remain and discharge their duty to him.

The Conclusion

What does God declare concerning all these Commandments?

Answer: He says: I the LORD thy God am a jealous God, visiting the iniquity of the fathers upon the children unto the third and fourth generation of them that hate Me; and showing mercy unto thousands of them that love Me and keep My commandments.

10

What does this mean?

Answer: God threatens to punish all who transgress these commandments. We should, therefore, fear His wrath, and in no wise disobey them. But He promises grace and every blessing to all who keep them. We should, therefore, love Him, trust in Him, and gladly keep His commandments.

PART II

THE CREED

The First Article

of creation

I believe in God the Father Almighty, Maker of heaven and earth.

What does this mean?

Answer: I believe that God has created me and all that exists; that He has given and still preserves to me my body and soul, my eyes and ears, and all my members, my reason and all the powers of my soul, together with food and raiment, home and family, and all my property; that He daily provides abundantly for all the needs of my life, protects me from all danger, and guards and keeps me from all evil; and that He does this purely out of fatherly and divine goodness and mercy, without any merit or worthiness in me; for all of which I am in duty bound

11

to thank, praise, serve, and obey Him. This is most certainly true.

The Second Article

OF REDEMPTION

And in Jesus Christ His only Son, our Lord; Who was conceived by the Holy Spirit, Born of the Virgin Mary; Suffered under Pontius Pilate, Was crucified, dead, and buried; He descended into hell; The third day He rose again from the dead; He ascended into heaven, And sitteth on the right hand of God the Father Almighty; From thence He shall come to judge the quick and the dead.

What does this mean?

Answer: I believe that Jesus Christ, true God, begotten of the Father from eternity, and also true Man, born of the Virgin Mary, is my Lord; Who has redeemed me, a lost and condemned creature, bought me and freed me from all sins, from death, and from the power of the devil; not with silver and gold, but with His holy and precious blood, and with His innocent sufferings and death; in order that I might be His own, live under Him in His kingdom, and serve Him in everlasting righteousness, innocence, and blessedness; even as He is risen from the dead, and lives and reigns to all eternity. This is most certainly true.

The Third Article

OF SANCTIFICATION

I believe in the Holy Spirit; The holy Christian Church, the Communion of Saints; The Forgiveness of sins; The Resurrection of the body; And the Life everlasting. Amen.

What does this mean?

Answer: I believe that I cannot by my own reason or strength believe in Jesus Christ my Lord, or come to Him; but the Holy Spirit has called me through the Gospel, enlightened me with His gifts, and sanctified and preserved me in the true faith; in like manner as He calls, gathers, enlightens, and sanctifies the whole Christian Church on earth, and preserves it in union with

14

Jesus Christ in the one true faith; in which Christian Church He daily forgives abundantly all my sins, and the sins of all believers, and at the last day will raise up me and all the dead, and will grant everlasting life to me and to all who believe in Christ. This is most certainly true.

PART III
THE LORD'S PRAYER

THE INTRODUCTION

Our Father, Who art in heaven.

What does this mean?

Answer: God thereby tenderly encourages us to believe that He is truly our Father, and that we are truly His children, so that we may boldly and confidently come to Him in prayer, even as beloved children come to their dear father.

THE FIRST PETITION

Hallowed be Thy Name.

What does this mean?

Answer: God's Name is indeed holy in itself; but we pray in this petition that it may be hallowed also among us.

15

How is this done?

Answer: When the Word of God is taught in its truth and purity and we, as God's children, lead holy lives, in accordance with it. This grant us, dear Father in heaven! But whoever teaches and lives otherwise than God's Word teaches, profanes the Name of God among us. From this preserve us, heavenly Father!

THE SECOND PETITION

Thy kingdom come.

What does this mean?

Answer: The kingdom of God comes indeed of itself, without our prayer; but we pray in this petition that it may come also to us.

How is this done?

Answer: When our heavenly Father gives us His Holy Spirit, so that by His grace we believe His holy Word, and live a godly life here on earth, and in heaven for ever.

THE THIRD PETITION

Thy will be done on earth, as it is in heaven.

What does this mean?

Answer: The good and gracious will of God is done indeed without our prayer; but we pray in this petition that it may be done also among us.

How is this done?

Answer: When God destroys and brings to naught every evil counsel and purpose of the devil, the world, and our own flesh, which would hinder us from hallowing His Name, and prevent the coming of His kingdom; and when He strengthens us and keeps us steadfast in His Word and in faith, even unto our end. This is His good and gracious will.

THE FOURTH PETITION

Give us this day our daily bread.

What does this mean?

Answer: God indeed gives daily bread to all men, even to the wicked, without our prayer; but we pray in this petition that He would lead us to acknowledge our daily bread as His gift, and to receive it with thanksgiving.

What is meant by daily bread?

Answer: Everything that is required to satisfy our bodily needs; such as food and raiment, house and home, fields and flocks, money and goods; pious parents, children, and servants; godly and faithful rulers, good government; seasonable weather, peace and health; order and honor; true friends, good neighbors, and the like.

THE FIFTH PETITION

And forgive us our trespasses, as we forgive those who trespass against us.

What does this mean?

Answer: We pray in this petition that our heavenly Father would not regard our sins nor because of them deny our prayers; for we neither merit nor are worthy of those things for which we pray; but that He would grant us all things through grace, even though we sin daily, and deserve nothing but punishment. And certainly we, on our part, will heartily forgive, and gladly do good to those who may sin against us.

The Sixth Petition

And lead us not into temptation.

What does this mean?

Answer: God indeed tempts no one to sin; but we pray in this petition that God would so guard and preserve us, that the devil, the world, and our own flesh, may not deceive us, nor lead us into error and unbelief, despair, and other great and shameful sins; but that, when so tempted, we may finally prevail and gain the victory.

The Seventh Petition

But deliver us from evil.

What does this mean?

Answer: We pray in this petition, as in a summary, that our heavenly Father would deliver us from all manner of evil, whether it affect body or soul, property or reputation, and at last, when the hour of death shall come, grant us a blessed end, and graciously take us from this world of sorrow to Himself in heaven.

The Conclusion

For Thine is the kingdom, and the power, and the glory, for ever and ever. Amen.

What does the word "Amen" mean?

Answer: It means that I should be assured that such petitions are acceptable to our heavenly Father, and are heard by Him; for He Himself has commanded us to pray in this manner, and has promised to hear us. Amen, Amen, that is, Yea, yea, it shall be so.

PART IV
THE SACRAMENT OF BAPTISM

I

WHAT IS BAPTISM?

Answer: Baptism is not simply water, but it is the water used according to God's command and connected with God's word.

What is this word of God?

Answer: It is the word of our Lord Jesus Christ, as recorded in the last chapter of Matthew: "Go ye therefore, and make disciples of all the nations, baptizing them into the Name of the Father and of the Son and of the Holy Spirit."

II

WHAT GIFTS OR BENEFITS DOES BAPTISM BESTOW?

Answer: It works forgiveness of sins, delivers from death and the devil, and gives everlasting salvation to all who believe, as the word and promise of God declare.

What is this word and promise of God?

Answer: It is the word of our Lord Jesus Christ, as recorded in the last chapter of Mark: "He that believeth and is baptized shall be saved; but he that disbelieveth shall be condemned."

III

How Can Water Do Such Great Things?

Answer: It is not the water, indeed, that does such great things, but the word of God, connected with the water, and our faith which relies on that word of God. For without the word of God, it is simply water and no baptism. But when connected with the word of God, it is a baptism, that is, a gracious water of life and a washing of regeneration in the Holy Spirit, as St. Paul says to Titus, in the third chapter: "According to His mercy He saved us, through the washing of regeneration and renewing of the Holy Spirit, which He poured out upon us richly, through Jesus Christ our Saviour; that, being justified by His grace, we might be made heirs according to the hope of eternal life. This is a faithful saying."

IV

WHAT DOES SUCH BAPTIZING WITH WATER SIGNIFY?

Answer: It signifies that the old Adam in us, together with all sins and evil lusts, should be drowned by daily sorrow and repentance, and be put to death; and that the new man should daily come forth and rise, to live before God in righteousness and holiness for ever.

Where is it so written?

Answer: St. Paul, in the sixth chapter of the Epistle to the Romans, says: "We were buried therefore with him through baptism into death: that like as Christ was raised from the dead through the glory of the Father, so we also might walk in newness of life."

OF CONFESSION

What is Confession?

Answer: Confession consists of two parts: the one is that we confess our sins; the other, that we receive absolution or forgiveness from the pastor as from God Himself, in no wise doubting, but firmly believing, that our sins are thereby forgiven before God in Heaven.

What sins should we confess?

Answer: Before God we should acknowledge ourselves guilty of all manner of sins, even of those of which we are not aware, as we do in the Lord's Prayer. To the pastor we should confess only those sins which we know and feel in our hearts.

What are such sins?

Answer: Here examine yourself in the light of the Ten Commandments, whether as father or mother, son or daughter, master or servant, you have been disobedient, unfaithful, slothful, ill-tempered, unchaste, or quarrelsome, or whether you have injured any one by word or deed, stolen, neglected, or wasted aught, or done any other evil.

PART V
THE SACRAMENT OF THE ALTAR

I

WHAT IS THE SACRAMENT OF THE ALTAR?

Answer: It is the true Body and Blood of our Lord Jesus Christ, under the bread and wine, given unto us Christians to eat and to drink, as it was instituted by Christ Himself.

Where is it so written?

Answer: The holy Evangelists, Matthew, Mark, and Luke, together with St. Paul, write thus:

"Our Lord Jesus Christ, in the night in which He was betrayed, took bread; and when He had given thanks, He brake it and gave it to His disciples, saying, Take, eat; this is My Body, which is given for you; this do in remembrance of Me.

"After the same manner, also, He took the

cup, when He had supped, and when He had given thanks, He gave it to them, saying, Drink ye all of it; this cup is the New Testament in My Blood, which is shed for you, and for many, for the remission of sins; this do, as oft as ye drink it, in remembrance of Me."

II

WHAT IS THE BENEFIT OF SUCH EATING AND DRINKING?

Answer: It is pointed out in these words: "Given and shed for you for the remission of sins." Through these words the remission of sins, life and salvation are given unto us in the Sacrament; for where there is remission of sins, there is also life and salvation.

III

HOW CAN THE BODILY EATING AND DRINKING PRODUCE SUCH GREAT BENEFITS?

Answer: The eating and drinking, indeed, do not produce them, but the words: "Given and shed for you for the remission of sins." For besides the bodily eating and drinking, these words are the chief thing in the Sacrament; and he who believes them has what they say and declare, namely, the remission of sins.

IV

WHO, THEN, RECEIVES THE SACRAMENT WORTHILY?

Answer: Fasting and bodily preparation are indeed a good outward discipline, but he is truly worthy and well prepared who believes these words: "Given and shed for you for the remission of sins." But he who does not believe these words or who doubts them is unworthy and unprepared; for the words: "For you," require truly believing hearts.

PRAYERS FOR VARIOUS OCCASIONS

MORNING PRAYERS

I thank Thee, my heavenly Father, that Thou hast kept me through the night from all harm and danger. I pray Thee to keep me this day from all sin and evil, that in all my thoughts and words and deeds I may serve and please Thee. Into Thy hands I commend my body and soul and all that is mine. Let Thy holy angels be with me, that the evil one may have no power over me. This I pray in Jesus' name.

Amen.

Jesus, friend of little children,
  Be a friend to me;
Take my hand and always keep me
  Near and dear to Thee.

Amen.

We are little children,
  Weak, and apt to stray;
Saviour, guide and keep us
  By Thy side today.

Amen.

Father, we thank Thee for the night,
And the pleasant morning light;
For rest and food and loving care,
And all that makes the day so fair.

Help us to do the things we should,
To be to others kind and good;
In all we do in work or play,
To grow more like Thee every day.
Amen.

EVENING PRAYERS

I thank Thee, my heavenly Father, that Thou hast graciously kept me all through this day. I pray Thee to forgive me all my sins and the wrong which I have done. By Thy great mercy keep me this night from all harm and danger. Into Thy hands I commend my body and soul, and all that is mine. Let Thy holy angels be with me, that the evil one may have no power over me. This I pray in Jesus' name.
Amen.

Now I lay me down to sleep,
I pray Thee, Lord, my soul to keep;
If I should die before I wake,
I pray Thee, Lord, my soul to take.
Amen.

Saviour, breathe an evening blessing,
Ere repose our spirits seal;
Sin and want we come confessing:
Thou canst save and Thou canst heal.
Amen.

A Mother's Evening Prayer for Her Child.

Sleep, my child, and peace attend thee
  All through the night.
Guardian angels God will send thee
  All through this night.
Soft the drowsy hours are creeping,
Hill and vale in slumber steeping;
I my loving watch am keeping
  All through the night.

Amen.

Prayers before Meals

Be present at our table, Lord;
Be here and everywhere adored.
These mercies bless, and grant that we
May feast in Paradise with Thee.

Amen.

Come, Lord Jesus, be our guest,
And let Thy gifts to us be blest.

Amen.

Break Thou the bread of life,
  Dear Lord, to me,
As Thou didst bless the bread
  By Galilee;
Give me to eat and live
  With Thee above;
Teach me to love Thy Truth,
  For Thou art love.

Amen.

PRAYERS AFTER MEALS

We thank Thee for our daily bread;
Let also, Lord, our souls be fed.
O Bread of Life, from day to day,
Sustain us on our homeward way.
Amen.

God is gracious, God is good,
We thank Him for our daily food.
Amen.

Heavenly Father, great and good,
We thank Thee for this daily food.
Bless us ever as we pray;
Guide and keep us through this day.
Amen.

PRAYERS OF PRAISE AND THANKSGIVING

Bless the Lord, O my soul,
And forget not all His benefits:
Who forgiveth all thine iniquities;
Who healeth all thy diseases;
Who crowneth thee with loving-kindness and
   tender mercies;
Who satisfieth thy desire with good things.
Amen.

Praise God, from whom all blessings flow;
Praise Him, all creatures here below;
Praise Him above, ye heavenly host;
Praise Father, Son, and Holy Ghost.
Amen.

A Prayer for Our Country

Our fathers' God, to Thee,
Author of liberty,
  To Thee we sing;
Long may our land be bright
With freedom's holy light;
Protect us by Thy might,
  Great God, our King.   *Amen.*

The Lord's Prayer

Our Father who art in heaven,
Hallowed be Thy name.
Thy kingdom come.
Thy will be done on earth as it is in heaven.
Give us this day our daily bread.
And forgive us our trespasses, as we forgive those
    who trespass against us.
And lead us not into temptation.
But deliver us from evil.
For Thine is the kingdom, and the power, and
    the glory, for ever.

                              Amen.

The Benediction

The Lord bless us and keep us,
The Lord make His face shine upon us and be
    gracious unto us.
The Lord lift up His countenance upon us and
    give us peace.
In the Name of the Father, and of the Son, and
    of the Holy Spirit.   *Amen.*